GOAL LARCENY

GOAL LARCENY

Awakening the love for Inner-Self

By

CARMEL PHARREL

Photography/Cover Design by Carmel Pharrel/Editing by
G. Virgoan

Passages in this book are a combination of fictional and
factual prospective of the author's life experiences in
Self-help, Personal Growth and Success. Results may
vary. All written content is solely to assist individuals to
get motivated. Under no circumstances is this book to be
used to treat or diagnose mental illnesses or other forms
of medical conditions. Seek the advice of a licensed
physician before practicing any vigorous forms of
dietary, physical or nutritional routines.

Contact Publisher with inquiries at

www.goallarcenycp.com

ISBN – 13: 978 – 1541329836

ISBN – 10: 154132983X

CARMEL PHARREL

Goal Larceny

Content

Acknowledgements

Introduction - The author's accounts of awakening the love for Inner-Self …. Pgs. 1-3

Goal Larceny - How to apply Goal Larceny to your life… Chapter 1 Pgs. 4-10

Grow a big head - Self-worth and ignoring the naysayer… Chapter 2 Pgs. 12-23

Affirmation Action - Using affirmations to obtain goals…Chapter 3 Pgs. 24-33

Get up off your ass - Scratch off tasks on your to-do list… Chapter 4 Pgs. 36-39

Don't be stingy - Pay it forward by helping others… Chapter 5 Pgs. 41-43

Bossed up -You are officially the boss… Chapter 6 Pgs. 45-47

Goal Larceny exercises and forms – Pgs. 52-56

About the Author - Pg. 57

Acknowledgement

This book is dedicated to my late mother Leona and our ancestors that are with her in spirit. Also to my beautiful children, my love, family and friends. I am strengthened by your sincere support. Thank you.

Introduction

Welcome to Goal Larceny a guidebook about

Awakening The love for Inner-Self. The intensions of the passages are to encourage people into completing goals. Rather it's upgrading your education, build up your self esteem, cleaning out the garage that's over cluttered, or wanting to own a business. Deep within you there is a goal larceny demon ready to be released and willing take you to the next level. But first, let me introduce myself.

I was born and raised in one of the toughest neighborhoods in the Bronx of New York City. An area where both newly developed apartment buildings stood alongside abandoned burnt complexes. Also where there was an increase in gang violence and drugs. As a young girl, my perspectives, at the time, were about playing with childhood friends, spending time with family and using my imagination as a form of entertainment. Nonetheless, oblivious that I was living within a destitute circumstance; which is said to be "the ghetto".

As a 70's baby, I grew up with a close-knit family and neighbors who looked out for one another. An unselfish community that pitched in as guardians or caregivers of each other's children and adults alike. If you needed a place to stay, food to eat or a babysitter it was obtainable. I can recall a time when I'd out grown my clothes and had been given shirts and pants which belonged to my next door neighbor's daughter who wore a size larger than me. Back in those days we called this exchange "hand me downs". Why throw away perfectly good garments when they can be passed down to a person in need? No wear and tear, no discoloration or revolting odors. As the saying goes "One man's trash is another man's treasure." Although, the area in which I had lived was among the poorest, the collectives still managed to maintain optimism. The smallest of gestures and people were respected with sincere gratitude.

There is an additional prime example on how "I can" has become a prominent root in my mind set and spirit. Not only by past experiences, but also by being taught. My number one goddess, encouraged me to always do my best. With eye to eye contact she said "There is no such thing as I can't." These are words of wisdom forever embedded in my heart. Sleep in peace Mom. I am now standing in strength as I continue to believe in my truths.

As I've gotten older it seems as if people are placing their fears on each other. Not cool. I remember a time when a Naysayer told me I couldn't start a business because I didn't have the money. That level of stupidity really angered me at first. Then I laughed. To own a business is what I wanted and I was well aware of my capabilities. So I got busy. Through proper planning, extensive research, I began the process of being a sole proprietor. Funding through grants and reimbursement programs

Introduction

helped with startup costs tremendously. With that being said, it has lead me to have owned a daycare home based business for over 2 years. I took a risk and made it happen. Did I stop there? No. Somehow I explored more "I can" ventures. The goal larcenist that I am interned for over four years in the independent music industry as a promoter, booking agent, and a short term manager.

After the beautiful experience of working in music, I've grown an interest to being a videographer. With little knowledge, I obtained certification at a local organization by attending low costs classes. I learned how to use television broadcasting equipment & now I am the Producer of my own TV show at their facility. "Madder Hatter Pro" is available on a public access channels. Check your TV channel guides for air times.

So without further or do, I thank the people who gave me the reason to prove to myself that I can do. I must confess, yes! I am positively guilty of Goal Larceny. Yes! I am guilty as charged of Awakening the Love for Inner-Self. I hope the person who is reading will be inspired. All that's required is to take one day at a time. Oh yeah, did I also mention that I am a breast cancer survivor, divorced and almost became homeless? I believed I could get through it and I did. Ready for that conversation about Awakening the Love for Inner-Self to committing Goal Larceny? Are you the ultimate Goal Larcenist?

CHAPTER 1

GOAL LARCENY

HOW TO APPLY GOAL LARCENY TO YOUR LIFE

Wake up! Your inner-self have been unloved entirely too long. Hindrance knocked on the door and became a squatter inside your temple. It has even invited its ruthless cousins fear, doubt and confusion. Ambushed and plainly robbed you of your devotedness, ideals and moxie. Get up and wash the crust out your eyes to look at yourself in the mirror to say "I am ready to live a healthy and prosperous life. Today I am in control of my thoughts, what I say and what I will do. I am committing to the crime of being the ultimate goal larcenist."

Denying oneself the satisfaction of reaching goals is like suffocating to death. The guilt upon you is the pillow of regrets placed over your face so you may never wake up to live. Holding on to the shoulda, woulda, coulda (should have, would have, could have) regret rope with a tight grip. Don't you believe it's about time to let go? Then you have the audacity to look towards outsiders for validation. Asking "What should I do?"; "What do you think?" Oh please stop it. You don't need permission or approval from anyone else. The answers you seek are within you. Be intuitive and confident with yourself. Then snatch what's rightfully yours. When the opportunity presents itself, take the golden moment to make goals a reality.

Do you ever find yourself daydreaming about the possibilities?

No time to waste. If your want it, go get it. There are no restraints on you. Visualize all that you desire. The universe is just as hungry for your positive energy as you are. It will happily throw back what you give it. What your hand dishes out is what you will receive. Manifestation is the overall objective. All it takes is your stillness, thoughts and conversation. Think of the universe as if it were your BFF and ride or die.

As humans, we have the natural sense to create worlds. Rather expressed in 3D visual effects, written in a book or played out before our very eyes in movies & television. No idea envisioned is stupid. Surely, there will be similarities, but we each produce a pinch of uniqueness. You will have a couple of failures along the way. Nevertheless, you still try to see what works and what doesn't. So does that really mean there's failure? The answer is no. As you read later you will understand 'why not' in depth.

Being a goal larcenist is a mindset that takes time to master, but is well worth it at the end. You are worthy to receive an abundant life. Your destiny is waiting for you to wake up. Think positively when entering the new and improved love for inner- self. Believe that all things are possible. But first, try these exercises that may help organize your mission to reaching your goals. There are 3 steps you can take to commit goal larceny:

1. Create a blueprint for your goals; 2. Scout the ins and outs; 3. Break in and grab goals.

Step #1

Creating a blueprint for your goals

The last I'd checked humans have brains. This very important organ is the almighty of the almightiest. A super highway for infinite amounts of information collected from the very beginning of conception. Do you have a brain? Of course you do.

Critical thinking is the first part of the process before drawing up your goal blueprint. At this point in time, you will ask yourself several questions: What is it that I'm passionate about? What are my strengths? How often have I utilized my skills? Who benefits from my abilities other than myself?

During this stage, try to avoid over thinking. The longer you pounder the faster you will begin to doubt. In some cases, maybe even lose interest in the process altogether. I for one, will not be an accessory to your over thinking. At least I advised you not to go that route. Then again, it goes back to the very person in the mirror. You will acknowledge your own accountability.

To make the blueprint for your goals official, write your goals, hopes or dreams down. Just like any form of writing this is the draft, your to do list for goals. This technique will keep you on focused on reaching goals. Writing enables you to see your progress and tasks that you have executed and what's next on the agenda.

Another possible way to assist you with goal completion is to create a vision board. All you need is your imagination, clue, markers, construction paper, and clippings from newspaper articles or magazines.

Arrange your visuals that describes the lifestyle you desire. For example, the house you want and where; the car you will be driving; the guy you wish to marry etc. When you paste your hopes and aspirations on the board don't forget include pictures of yourself. You may want to introduce this method to friends and family too. It's a really fun activity for anyone looking to reach goals.

Step #2

Scouting the ins and outs

The next step is to case your place in the world. Seek all the necessary resources that will enhance your knowledge in the subjects. Today's society is full of open sources of information, technologies and training programs. We are fortunate to have multitudes of resourcefulness at our disposal.

In addition to seeking resources, it's imperative to ask questions. There's no such thing as a stupid question. Make the phone calls, send out emails or simply get up and go. Take advantage of the people who have reached their career goals and get their advice. No matter the age, it's never too late to seek a mentor. One thing I've learned on my crime spree to goal larceny is that people are generous with their resourcefulness and advice. Sort of their way of paying it forward. (You'll have the chance to learn more about paying it forward later on in the chapters)

Ultimately, casing your options, is to research listings of workshops in the field of interest. Local libraries, colleges and resource centers usually conducts little to no cost sessions. Professionals are often the instructors or guest speakers at these events. Be prepared to enter with an open mind and leave with a bag full of goodies. Reading materials, free promotional products and extended course information are given to participants.

Step #3

Breaking in and grabbing goals

Everything you ever wanted is right in view. Be strategic, but yet charismatic when scaling down the walls to successfully reaching goals. Believe in your progression. Give your inner-self a swift kick to the throat if it begins to corrupt you with negative thoughts, feelings and talks.

Procrastination and excuses are the worst accomplices while trying to commit goal larceny. These two will demoralize your abilities. They are known for mulishly coercing people from self- love altogether. Don't become their victim. Do you love yourself? Like I stated earlier (in so many words) you can be your own worst enemy.

Get caught red handed by grabbing opportunities. To be a business owner, a song writer or director of films you must GRAB IT; Snatch it up. Closing your eyes and blowing out the candles, while making a wish on your birthday just doesn't cut it these days. Do what you need or want to do.

All and all, grow accustomed to being grateful for what you now have. That way, when there's an overflow of blessings you won't trigger anxiety. With prosperity comes more responsibilities. If you should find yourself loosing a grip on achieving goals, know it's a part of your divine plan. The good coexists with the bad. The bad, of course, is temporary. At the end of the day, that's life. That is **goal larceny**.

10

Goals are shackled to my feet & positive beliefs are worn like a nap sap strapped to my back. I honor such a privilege.

– Carmel Pharrel

CHAPTER 2

GROW A BIG HEAD

SELF WORTH & IGNORING THE NAYSAYERS

Let us dig a little deeper as I take you into the inner world of self. By no means is this chapter set up to kick a person while they're down. Nor is it intended to offend. Nevertheless, I hope that whoever is reading these words can use them as a pick-me-up.

In today's society, we as a nation are dealing with daily pressures of life. From maintaining lavish lifestyles, careers, taking care of our families and praying to be able to afford basic necessities. Repugnant news coverage doesn't help make the situation any better. With consistent reports about deadly shootings, terrorism and horrible politics. Our planet is showing signs of distress. Unusual weather patterns are causing drought, tornadoes, and catastrophic tsunamis. In result, a slew of people are living in unimaginable conditions or as of now deceased.

At some point your mind becomes full of uncertainty and fear. You begin questioning your self worth to focusing on your flaws. Yes, I understand your mental frustrations and empathize completely. Now, the question is how will you combat the negatives and remain steadfast in positivity? I say **grow a big head.**

To grow a big head is to have confidence and undoubtedly know that things will be ok. Think back to when your teeth began to fall out as a kid. The pain every time you tried to eat your favorite meals and you couldn't. Those teeth had to be pulled. There was blood, but there was also a sigh of relief. Your gums healed and teeth grew back stronger than they were before. Well, my dear worry wart, as you can see you got through it. Better yet, you lived to tell about it. That's a key example how life is and how each day you will have to reinsure yourself that things will be alright. Life goes on.

I'm sure there are a few other scenarios of trails that you may have encountered and won the battles. Rather from being diagnosed with a deadly disease like cancer, having your house foreclosed or losing money in the stock market. There had been a better blessing that came along after the storm. Now the sun is shining and you're smiling today. Tell your story about how you got over. As the spiritual faith communities believe, we are living testimonies. Sometimes you have to sacrifice one blessing for another in order to obtain the main blessing. Pain comes with pleasure. Unfortunately, it's seemingly impossible to have one without the other.

Are any of us exempt from negativity? No. A spark has to come from somewhere. A rude awakening has to happen to get the positive going. So please don't be naive in thinking otherwise. This doesn't mean to cause affliction to anyone else. If you are a serial killer or in a cult, please drop this book and seek some professional help. I'm not in the business to encouraging the wicked. No sir, not at all.

Growing a big head will take you to where you're destined to be. Having fortitude eases the tensions of fighting against oneself. Let confidence be seen in your posture. Let your confidence be heard as you give a lecture. Let your confidence be you. In no way, shape or form does this means to belittle others. That is not confidence.

Somehow, people have a misconceived notion of confidence being egotistical or downright rude. Individuals who grow big heads are about love for self and practicality. If you happen to be a bully, you're most definitely in need of some serious self-love consultations. Unresolved issues are tearing your soul apart. Once your mentality positively improves we'll gladly welcome you with open arms. All are welcomed to join us on this journey. Until then we'll keep your seat warm. Get help.

Fear has been identified as the culprit sabotaging people's lives. There are ways to combat this invader that wins its way into the minds of many. It's time to whip fear's butt and send it packing. I have listed several solutions to the fear problem that may assist you. Believe you are deserving of having a successful, fearless life. Ready to grow a big head? Here's how:

1. Write down your strengths. Analyze how those strengths benefited your life in the past as well as presently. Think about your accomplishments. If you have awards, honors or photographs, pull them out and look at them. How about placing them in plain view so they're a constant reminder of how well you're doing. Go ahead and gloat. Why not?

2. Stay clear of pessimistic people. They have a tendency to be unhappy with just about everything. You say "good morning." They'd say "what's so good about it?" You say "smile." They'd say "what for?" These obnoxious people lack empathy about

the well-being of others. Pessimistic people are bitter and life to them seems worthless. As the saying goes "misery loves company". Get rid of them. You don't need their doom and gloom rubbing off on you. Tell em' "Poof! Be gone killjoy."

3. Turn off the television and other devices that are distracting you. As I stated before the news reports are saturated with bad news. So are other social media outlets. The ratchet string of events seems to become a way of life and very acceptable. Guard your emotions and just simply do away with the manipulations. You'll feel much better.

4. Clean your house. People that are showing signs of depression tend to not clean their homes and have clutter throughout the house. They accumulate papers, shop a lot and leave a huge mess. If by any means you are experiencing these signs severely, please drop this book and seek professional help immediately. Nevertheless, keep reading if you are just going through a temporary case of confusion.

To begin the steps to be uncluttered is to tackle the large piles first. See what's relevant. No use in keeping items that are just going to sit around and collect dust. Once the task of cleaning house is completed, your mind should be much clearer.

5. Detoxify, exercise or mediate. These activities work wonders. To detoxify is to rid impurities in the major organs and in the blood. As you cleanse, the entire body becomes healthier. Meditation conditions the mind, body and spirit as well. When doing so you combine calmness with a series yoga positions. Find a quiet place to relax and control your breathing. Think of a place that makes you happy. This method is bringing you deeper within yourself. To be one with self is to know thyself. Meditation is an ancient practice used for all sorts of ailments and various religions.

6. Find an activity that makes you feel good. I am confident that you have something that get's you in a feel good

mood. Give yourself that spark by getting into a hobby of some sorts. Rather it is painting, photography, going to your favorite karaoke bar to sing your heart out, get going. Whatever you decide to do it's meant to be enjoyed. Self-gratification is a gateway to a better smile, higher vibrations and a better you.

7. When was the last time you pampered yourself? Turn on your favorite tunes and draw up a bubble bath. Add some essential oils like lavender or a fragrance of your choice. There are a variety of soothing products on the market for an aching body and stress. The great thing about it, they're inexpensive and conveniently sold in discount to major department stores. Maybe

you would prefer to go to a spa with all the services of rejuvenation. Get a 45 minute head to toe body massage, steam or detoxification wrap. If you have the means to splurge and would like take advantage of a full day package do it. At the end of the day you will be refreshed, relaxed and vibrant.

8. Take yourself out on a date. Make reservations at a restaurant that you been dying to try. Dig in back of your closet and pull out the special occasion outfit. Throw on your favorite perfume or cologne. Call up a taxi service and enjoy much needed me time. A play, movie or a day at the beach, it doesn't matter. There's nothing like a date by yourself for yourself. Alone time can work wonders.

9. Traveling seemly does the trick in addition. You find yourself doing everything for everyone but yourself. Find a destination that suits you. It doesn't necessarily have to be the most lavish and expensive trip either. Maybe you can make a reservation to a nearby hotel. Often time's hotels have conventions, parties and other amenities that can be an addition to your stay. Take advantage of all there is to offer. Have that breakfast in bed and melt all your troubles away. This is a great way to release, relax and regroup. After it's all said and done, your mind should be on the how blessed you are and not on things you're unable to control. Come back into the world with a new attitude.

10. Stop comparing yourself with others. When there is comparison involved there are expectations. This takes away from self love and causes

doubt, worry, and fear. Avoid the downward spiral. It is not good for what ails you to embracing your goals. How can you grow or achieve goals in life if you are busy looking into the lives of others? Focus on what is meant for you and your strengths. Show gratitude for all you have and for what's to come.

CHAPTER 3

AFFIRMATION ACTION

USING AFFIRMATIONS TO OBTAIN GOALS

Affirmations are conscious and subconscious thoughts or words spoken in which will manifest. They are usually negatively or positively used on a daily basis. However, the true objective of affirmations is to focus on the positives.

Essentially, affirmations are a powerful tool that works in conjunction with reaching goals. It will attract the right people, opportunities and will respond in your favor. As you begin to write, use words in their presentence. Your emotions are the vibration of your truths. Hopefully, you have already addressed any self esteem issues or fears before you begin using affirmations. This way you are free from negativity and road blocks that will hinder your desires. You are in the state of a positive subconscious mind and can move forward to being the winner that you are.

Be deliberate and present while writing down your affirmations. Start with the words "I am". For example, you're working at a major department store as a stock person for over 4 years and believe that you deserve a raise. Write down an affirmation that states "I am an excellent manager and deserve an increase in my income." List more "I am" affirmations and recite them for approximately 5 minutes daily. Store your list in a safe place and don't share it with anyone. What's for you is for you.

Be careful sharing your goals and dreams. Not everyone is happy for you nor do they want you to succeed. Haters are just as real and more often the main ones who will manipulate a situation so that it doesn't work in your favor. Nevertheless, you can pass on the information about the use of affirmations and testify how well the method works for you.

I have put together a list of 100 affirmations that will help you get started. Remember to stay positive throughout the journey. Keep yourself in the state of great confidence, make gratitude the ultimate attitude and remain fearless in your approach.

1   I am strong and balanced.
2   I am like a strong tree whose roots are deeply connected to mother earth.
3   I am courage and strength.
4   I am inner peace.
5   I am protected by my higher self.
6   I am open to love, laughter and a fun life.
7   I am flexible to change.
8   I am free to do whatever I love.

9   I am grateful for all of my needs.

10 I am a magnet for abundance.

11 I am positive in my thoughts.

12 I am deserving of prosperity.

13 I am worthy of the finest things in life.

14 I am thankful for the flow of good in my life.

15 I am surrounded by money.

16 I am the power behind my destiny.

17 I am abundantly healthy in my mind, body and spirit.

18 I am successful.

19 I am a top motivator who believes that there's no such thing as a box.

20 I am highly driven and can accomplish whatever I put my mind to.

21 I am focused.

22 I attract people and situations that will help me.

23 I am beautiful in every way.

24 I am illumination.

25 I am radiant.

26 I am plenty.

27 I am a champion of ambition.

28 I am unlimited.

29 I am open-minded.

30 I am attractive.

31 I am divinely guided.

32 I am blissful.

33 I am a billionaire.

34 I am beautifully blessed.

35 I am grace.

36 I am secure in my thoughts.

37 I am the truth.

38 I am full in wisdom.

39 Great wealth is flowing to me now.

40 Everyday and in every way I am becoming more prosperous.

41 My greatest good is coming to me now.

42 I am wide awake to my abundance.

43 Wealth is my birthright.

44   Whatever I do it always attracts abundant wealth.

45   Today is full of opportunity and I will seize it.

46   Everything is coming to me easily and effortlessly.

47   I know there's ample prosperity for all.

48   I let go of all resistance to prosperity.

49   I release resistance about wealth.

50   I am extremely successful.

51   I share my prosperity freely with the world.

52   I expect the best and I live it now.

53   Abundance and I are one.

54   The universe has chosen me to be wealthy so I can help others achieve the same.

55   I automatically receive money in abundance.

56   I am living the life of my wealthy dreams.

57 Whatever activities I perform will make me money.

58 My ideas are incredible and I have the creative energy to bring them to life.

59 The more abundantly I live the more abundance I will receive.

60 If others can be wealthy so can I.

61 My bank balance is increasing everyday.

62 Unexpected large amount of income attracted to me.

63 Each day my life is full of wonders and magic.

64 The seeds of great wealth are inside me.

65 I am a healer and full of great faith.

66 Positive energy is in abundance in my life.

67 I am in a constant state of fulfillment.

68 It is so easy for me to become wealthy.

69   I am proud of my accomplishments.

70   No one can talk me out of my highest goal.

71   I appreciate those who love me.

72   I embrace my passions.

73   I believe that I have the power to succeed.

74   I am a gift to the world.

75   I have enormous confidence in myself.

76   Writing down my goals challenges me.

77   Every cell of my body is healthy.

78   The more I apply myself the more I achieve.

79   I can, I am able and I will achieve.

80   I speak from my heart.

81   Nothing is impossible.

82   I maintain my health and honor my body.

83   Abundance manifest in all my affairs.

84   I live in harmony with my higher self.

85   My power is in the present moment.

86   There is no such thing as I can't.

87   It's so easy being who I am.

88   I love and approve of myself.

89   I release all regrets of my past.

90   Everyday I wake up with an empowered mind.

91   Self pitty and worry is always replaced by ultimate love for myself.

92   I am a true believer that life is to be lived and enjoyed.

93   I am unique and a gift to the people around me.

94   I release all thoughts that doesn't serve me well.

95   I will not listen to the Naysayers. I choose to trust and only listen to myself.

96   Unimportant things are released from my life.

97 I choose to make happiness my number one goal in my life.

98 I am on a wonderful path to a life full of love.

99 My inner wisdom is strongly trusted at all times.

100 I am the perfect go getter and ultimate goal larcenist.

Turbulence shakes and awakens you. A good fair weather friend. – Carmel Pharrel

CHAPTER 4

GET UP OFF YOUR ASS

SCRATCH OFF TASKS ON YOUR TO-DO LIST

Your to do list is not going to take care of itself. What do you think? Do you have it mind that after you have cleverly conjured up a brilliant set of goals and that's all there is to it? Think again. The Key words are TO DO. It's time for some tough love.

Goal setting is one thing, but if you don't apply the physical energy into the mix, your list of goals are just words on paper. I personally prefer not to engage in the "all talk with no action" lifestyle. Stagnated people, in my opinion, are wasting their precious lives away. To make excuses constantly in life and miss out on exploring endless possibilities is unfortunate. Not to say that this is exactly the case for yourself. I'm certain that you're just in need of an extra push to get started. The generous, kind hearted person that I am wants to see people win.

Do you believe you are a winner? Of course you do. However, you are in need of some tough love and I am honored to oblige you. Ready? Get up off your ass and go get it! It's about time that you squash the doubt bug that whispers in your ear. Take charge of your own life. Analyze your situation and make the necessary adjustments. Dig within the depths of your being and love yourself more. Self love is better than artificial love any day. Say to yourself "I have all going great for me and I am grateful for my life". Complete these spoken words with an acceptable belief that this is a fact.

Jump on your own band wagon and feel wonderful about it today. The past is gone. Old habits, bad relationships and the house of madness. Do away with it all. How do you expect the new prosperous you if you are holding on to the things that had you in a hot mess from the get? Let it go! Keep the good memories. Learn from any mistakes you made and be presently happy. Believe, Believe, Achieve, Achieve! The only thing you would want to go back to is the beginning of this guidebook. Read the passages again until your thought process has strengthened.

Pace yourself, there's no use in rushing. Start with a small goal and see how the power within resonates. The source and supply are within. You are all you need. Stop looking for answers on the outside. Be fully present in your being. Your best life is unfolding right now. Yes right now! Breathe easy and allow yourself to freely love you. Clear your mind and emotions. Then create a world of all that's due to you. Stimulate and awaken the spirit. Fly higher than you've ever had. Blossom, then live a life in abundance.

You want that new car with the shiny rims? Get up off your ass and go get it! Do you want a 4 bedroom, 2 full baths and huge walk-in closets featured home? Get up off your ass and go get it! You worked all year long and never missed a day. So you're saying to yourself "I deserve a 2 weeks vacation". There's a relative that you haven't spoken to in years because of a huge misunderstanding. You wish to put the pettiness to the side and regain a loving relationship with them. Get up off your ass and go get it! Missed several Sunday services at your church and praying to god to give you strength to attend soon. You want to the word. What you going to do? ... Need I say more?

Whatever you desire is already there. You may not be able to put a finger on it, but it's already there. Be your own genie. Trust yourself. Love yourself. Nurture yourself. Believe in yourself. Manifestation overflows as well as the creator who joyously visualizes their inner rise. You feel that you are greater than where you are at the moment. Know that it's your truth. Now get up off your ass and go get it! Stay beautifully blessed.

No reserved seating for my enemies of
my inner-me

--Carmel Pharrel

CHAPTER 5

DON'T BE STINGY

PAY IT FORWARD BY HELPING SOMEONE ELSE

Congratulations! You have learned to be the best goal larcenist on the planet. All your power should be bursting through your pores. A fragrance of strawberries should fill the air as the wind blows gently across your skin. The universe is ready to respond to your calls for abundance. Your senses are awakened and ravished with wisdom more than ever before. Confidence levels are at its highest point. You are currently aware that nothing happens accidently. Accepting, the role as the creator of your reality. Can you now handle the task of passing down this truth to the next person? Of course you can. That my friend is how you pay it forward.

Paying it forward is simple. All you're doing is helping the next person succeed. It may be by donating money, assisting them with their business ideas or even telling them about this goal larceny guidebook. The tiniest action you bless the next individual or groups of people with is adding more honor upon yourself. Do unto others as you do unto self. The universe will shower you with additional prosperity.

Don't be stingy with your treasures. Assist others on their road to building up self-confidence and love for inner-self. Corrupt their minds every chance you get. However, do so humbly and positively. Don't be that zealous person we spoke about in the previous chapters. Be your authentic, genuine self.

Everyone loves givers and everyone loves to receive. Our give and take world on this here planet can be used for the greater good of its people. This is possible as each one of us wake up and embrace our birthright. Yourself. Only then we will be able to band together to raise the vibrations to its highest peek. The power doesn't belong to just one person alone. It belongs to the entire race.

As for myself, I don't know how many people I will inspire once they have read this book, but I am confident that it will. In fact, it is not my job to know the results. Nevertheless, it's up to the people to hold themselves accountable for choosing the course of action by taking in consideration of the suggestive texts.

Reconditioning the mind of others boils down to compassion and empathy. Everyone has a story and can relate to the hardships. They too may have experienced homelessness, grew up without a mother or father, been bullied in school or didn't have proper clothing during freezing winter months. Praying to the heavens to come out of theses situations unscathed with goals of great success. That spark was ignited and lead them to a better lifestyle. Allowing them to live out their wildest dreams.

We were not born to work to death in order to live. We are here to live with the use of our works. To exercise our purpose. Continue to awaken the love for inner self and continue to spread wealth of knowledge to the masses. Most importantly, pay it forward with humility.

The greatest spark comes from the one
who set ablaze the torch of another.

– Carmel Pharrel

CHAPTER 6

BOSSED UP

YOU ARE OFFICIALLY THE BOSS

Job titles is what an owner of a company uses to define their workers. A label in which tricks an employee into feeling of great importance. The awakened people who define themselves within know it's bogus. An employer is not the boss of you, you are.

Don't' believe the hype. We know once the owner uses up all your devoted time and energy they lay you off. Pulling the rug up right from under your feet. Can you imagine what it would be like to have worked vigorously for over 25 years for a company and get laid off because the company is being relocated overseas? Or a company merged with another company and they have to cut costs? All they can say to you is thank you for your dedication. Well not with the new inner you. You're bossed up and ready to take on whatever is thrown your way.

Micromanage yourself to the place where no one or nothing can detour you from your goals. If you come across others that are able to be an asset to your enterprise, let them assist. Those are your board members. Remember you attract people, places and things by your thoughts and from what you speak.

Divine intelligence which dwells are no longer in vain. Circulating a flow of prosperity, accountability and leadership. A force to be reckon with that surely takes guts. Charisma attached to a flame made difficult to extinguish. Once you are a boss it's hard for anyone to run game on you. Their body language, aura and energy reaches you way before they open their mouth. People can advise or suggest to you, but never should they try to tell you what you to do. I don't care who it is, we all learn, live and breathe at a different pace. One of my pet peeves is seeing how the next person dictates and judge people. Gets under my skin. Besides, your destiny won't allow that nonsense anyway. Your mind. Your body. Your spirit. Your life. It's all about you. Beware of the "You better" "You should be" and "I told you to" types of people, but I don't have to tell you that. Go do your thing, boss.

The path you choose should be enjoyable, not a burden

- Carmel Pharrel

Wreck'n Wall

I dreamt of being determined to demolish a dead end wall.
A wall which stood 20 feet high and almost three states
wide. Despite what others might had thought, I knew for a
fact I was going through that wall. Low on money in hand
and a negative balance to my account wouldn't stop me.
Even if I had to scrape up and barter my way to glory, that
wall was coming down. Remarkably, I had the support of a
few who helped me pay for the destructive machine. Oh
the joys of sticking the key in the ignition and as I pulled
the lever to begin the demolition. The beastly, huge black
wrecking ball hit with explosive force and had the sound of
a thousand running elephants. Piles of brick and dust
scattered in different directions. I seen hope, I seen
freedom. There in plain view was a gaping hole with a
bright illumination. Hell, I felt so satisfied I gave myself a
standing ovation. I felt so empowered and happy about
this phenomenon. I decided to take a break before I
moved on. First to rejoice in small victory with a sip of a
cold glass of lemonade that a sweet old lady had given me.
I turned away just for a moment to smile at the on lookers
who once thought that it would be impossible to remove
such a dreadful wall. Their attempts in the past hadn't
gotten close to what I had accomplished, not at all. Some
bystanders showed signs of relief, while others had a look
of disgust and grief. Almost as if they knew something that
I didn't. Not phased and a shrug of my shoulders I was
too smitten. Gulped the last of my drink then turned

around. To my amazement, that monstrosity of a wall was intact. It appeared as if it hadn't been broken at all. Then my sleep was abruptly interrupted by loud music playing from my alarm clock. Can you guess what song that was? It would have helped if the song was about a helicopter. Oh what a day.

GOAL LARCENY

What are your goals? & What are the time frames you would like to complete them?

Goals	Time Frame

CARMEL PHARREL

TO-DO LIST

_____

_____

_____

_____

_____

_____

_____

_____

_____

GOAL LARCENY

Write you own affirmations

What are your strengths?

List your accomplishments

About the author

Carmel Pharrel is a mother of three who resides in her hometown New York City. Carmel volunteers her services to community, participates in charity events and is an advocate for children.

Carmel Pharrel is an independent producer of her current public access show *Madder Hatter Pro* and is gearing up to participate in various film festivals. Carmel will also be introducing a podcast.

 You may find Carmel Pharrel in attendance among a crowd of celebrities, independent artists and a variety of festive outings. Ultimately, wherever there's a unique story to capture. As Carmel Pharrel would say "To go bonkers is insanely genius."

Goal Larceny, Awakening The Love for Inner-Self is Carmel's 1st book in which reflects her charismatic nature to motivate and inspire others. The book itself is opening up a conversation about self-love and what it may take to maintain it. Goal Larceny is now available in paperback and will also be available in audiobook form. Surely, you can expect further great reads written by the author in the near future.

57

GOAL LARCENY

CARMEL PHARREL

GOAL LARCENY

Made in the USA
Middletown, DE
23 March 2017